First Love

First Love

Brad Ringer

ISBN: 1539847535
ISBN 13: 9781539847533

Contents

Acknowledgments

I would like to thank the following people from the bottom of my heart. They have helped shape *First Love*.
Thank you Emma, Dawnette, Linda, and Deb.

A special thanks to my daughter Bonnie who during the creation process, helped to lift the chains off when I felt weighed down.

Introduction

If there is one thing that burns in my brain and guides me as I write this, it is that you would come to meet, then know, and finally fall in love with the risen Jesus. Then after you fall in love with Him, entrusting your heart to Him to make you into a person whose life pleases God.

We live in an age where so many people claim they have met Jesus, but their lives, their actions, their values and their words look nothing like Him. There are many who know of or about Jesus; but this knowledge is only academic or is a memory. Some claim to know Jesus, but this means little when their lives look like everybody else's around them.

Listen to this statement: **If you truly knew Jesus and what He's done for you, you could not help but fall deeply and passionately in love with Him.** In other words when you experience firsthand the love that Jesus has for you, it will transform your life. How?

You will be able to love the unlovable, like Jesus does.
You'll start forgiving the unforgivable.
You'll begin to hate sin, fakery, and religion.
Your heart will become pure, not dragged down by the immoral crud all around you.
You will start to experience joy that comes from God, not from things.
Jesus's presence in you will alter the moods of those around you.
You'll take on Jesus's realness in humility.
You will know the deep urge Jesus had to obey and please His Father God.
Because of His faithfulness to you, you will start to desire to be faithful to the commitments you have made.
You will start to seek to please God in every area of your life.
You'll pray, and like Jesus, when you do pray, things will be moved.

It is not possible to meet someone who was sinless, lived a perfect life, was crucified by His enemies and yet forgave them, forgave you, took away the punishment for every sin you have ever committed and after being murdered came back to life three days later…and not be filled with wonder. There are individuals who have no sense of wonder, who claim to know about Jesus, but prove they do not because they fail to love Him deeply. Without a sense of wonder, church, religious activities, Bible reading, prayer and Christian "stuff" grow boring and pointless. This cannot be hidden or fixed by exciting worship singers, comfortable instead of respectful environments, or fluff. When I was sixteen, I met the risen Jesus Christ, and today He is my first love. One day I was traveling on a plane from New York to Amsterdam. As I sat there, I spent almost the entire seven hours thinking about what Jesus went through on the cross for me.

I thought about His **crown of thorns**.

It symbolized how my evil and hate-filled thoughts put Jesus on the cross.

I pictured His **eyes beaten and swollen shut**.

They represented my lustful glances, jealous stares, and angry glares at people. He was killed for those too!

I imagined His **ears, cut and swollen**.

I thought of all lies and gossip I have listened to in my life. They hung Him there.

I saw His **dried, cracked, and dehydrated lips.**

I could not count the number of hurtful and crude things that have poured out of my mouth. He was sentenced to death by them.

I pictured His **loins**.

I was overwhelmed with all the times I had entertained impure thoughts. And He was hung naked and publicly humiliated, over my private thoughts.

I thought about His **legs, twisted, mangled, and disjointed.**

I thought of all the times I could've taken a stand for Him, but I wimped out.

In my mind I went to His **pierced and bloody feet.**

I remembered innumerable times my feet had taken me to places where my being there could bring no honor to God.

I then focused on His **nail-pierced hands.**

I began to think how my hands had been habitually used to sin. By this time I was crying.

And finally, I pictured the **spear hole into His heart.**

I fully admitted it was *my* sin that had broken Jesus's heart.

Then I thought of Romans 5:6–8:

> *"You see at just the right time, when we were still powerless, **Christ died for the ungodly**. Very rarely will anyone die for a righteous man, though for a good man someone might possibly dare to die. But **God demonstrated His own love** for us in this; while we were still sinners, **Christ died for us."***

Your thoughts, lusts, sin, disobedience, improper relationships, gossip, faithlessness, lies, and disrespect and ingratitude toward Him are the very sins that hung Him up on the cross. Yes! He still loves you! Owning this truth is a necessary first step to you being made right with God.

How could anyone love me this much as to die for me? But He did. Have you heard the song *Amazing Grace*? It has been sung by millions through time who know the words but do not understand them.

> *"Amazing grace how sweet the sound, that saved a wretch like me.*
> *I once was lost, but now I am found, was blind but now I see!"*

x

You cannot accept Jesus Christ as your personal Savior, and never be in awe of Him, His love, and forgiveness for you that He demonstrated on the cross. **IF YOU HAVE NEVER HAD A SENSE OF WONDER ABOUT JESUS… YOU HAVE NEVER MET HIM!**

The day you truly fall in love with Jesus is the day you are no longer spiritually blind. In John chapter nine there's a story of a man who had been blind since birth. Jesus healed his blindness. Later that day people asked him, "How is this possible?" The man simply replied, "I don't know, but one thing I can tell you, I once was blind but now I see!"

A man was riding on a bus one day, going through a derelict part of town. It was a hot and muggy day and everybody was complaining, except this one man. He kept saying "Wow! Look how beautiful!" Finally someone asked him what was so beautiful, as this part of town was ugly. He simply responded, "Three days ago I had surgery. I had been blind since birth, but a great doctor restored my sight. This is the first day I am able to see in my entire life! Everything I see is beautiful."

That is how you see God and life after Jesus comes into your life. Everything becomes new—everything. There is no part of you He leaves unchanged. He becomes your first love. That is my prayer for you as you go through this study; that you will meet Jesus, know Jesus, and then fall deeply and passionately in love with Him.

Can you say this? Was there a time when all of a sudden you came to know you were a sinner, condemned by sin, to a life of not being able to see God? But then you met Jesus. He took away your sins, opened your spiritual eyes, and now you can see God?

As you begin I would like to share with you writing from my heart entitled "BEAUTIFUL GOD."

BEAUTIFUL GOD

God, You are unrivaled in appearance. You are beautiful.
When my heart is sinful, You gently wash me.
In times of health, I see Your beauty.
In illness You put on a nurse's apron and stick by my bed.
Your beauty permeates every one of Your titles;
beautiful Lord, beautiful Savior, beautiful Creator.
The beauty of Your forgiveness is without end.
Beautiful God,
a very beautiful God.
Unresolved questions I have about life sink into Your beauty.
Because of Your beauty anyplace with You is beautiful.
Your beauty is deeper than life's harshest offerings.
By having faith, I've tasted Your beauty.
The beauty of being able to trust without seeing or knowing.
Your beauty attracts me.
You have mercy when my life is uglied by sin.
Jesus Your beauty is uncut, undivided, exhaustive,
and without flaw.
You hold a leper, and heal the blind beggar.
Yet at the same time expel fakes from your Father's house.
Your truth is beautiful.
For You are the truth, the whole truth,
and nothing but the truth.

Father, make Yourself beautiful in me.
Not that I would be attractive others,
but that You could be seen in me!
I love You beautiful God.

"You will seek me and find me when you seek me with all your heart." (Jer. 29:13)

This is the beginning, the starting point.

It makes sense that if we say we want to know and experience God, yet everything is about what we can get out of the experience, or if our eyes are on the people or things around us then we will walk away every time with unanswered questions, missed encounters with God, and doubt.

Let's imagine we have only heard about and seen pictures of the ocean. You've heard stories of swimmers and surfers, the salty sea water, and building sand castles on a hot day. It all sounds great, so you decide to go in and experience the ocean for yourself and to bring a part of it back with you. How much of the ocean will you walk away with?

You're on the way to the beach and you come across people talking about their time at the beach, or a group of musicians singing songs about the ocean. They may even be handing out cups of ocean water as they tell you how powerful the surf on the beach is. Are you willing to stop your trek there? Will you be satisfied with your experience? Are you willing to take away only what they offer about what they know about the beach? Or are you going to roll out a beach towel, put on your bathing suit, lather on sunscreen, and take pictures? Would you post your pictures showing and telling everyone what a great time you're having at the beach? (#nofilter) If this is what you did, would you really take any of the ocean home with you, or just memories?

If you show up at the ocean unprepared to carry anything away, you may only walk away with a little residual on your clothes and skin. Maybe you bring with you a paper cup or a coffee mug. You still can take away only what you are prepared to take away. You always have the opportunity to take away as much as you want. It is not the ocean's fault if you walk away with little or nothing. The same can be true when you approach God. Because you were unprepared to take the ocean away, likewise, **it is not God's fault when you walk away with nothing of Him.**

Many people get nothing from God because that is all they are prepared to take away. They do religious things and go to religious places, but they do not experience all of God. Some aim for just enough of Him to get help with some problems they're facing. Maybe they go to church to appease others like parents or peers. Some even go so they can feel good about themselves, by hearing inspiring stories, and music, or enjoy people who talk about a God that they themselves have never met. Many people approach God never expecting or believing that God will forgive them, talk to them, expand their thinking, talk to them about their future or change their lives. Some are content listening to people tell stories and sing songs about their experiences with God, but others, perhaps you, wonder what is missing and why you don't have your own experience to share.

I once heard said that Christians don't often tell lies, but they sing them all the time. **The only way to find God is to seek Him intensely through His son Jesus Christ.** If you look to people for your "God fix," you will walk away with nothing. If you are focused on yourself when you approach God, you will not be prepared to walk away with any of Him. If all you ever do is listen to other people's stories about God, and don't seek after Him yourself, all you will do is walk away with other people's memories.

With God, just like the ocean, I found the best way to enjoy Him is to just jump in with all your heart, mind, soul, and enthusiasm. What did He say? *"You will seek me and find me, when you seek me with all your heart"* (Jer. 29:13). Have you been seeking God enthusiastically and with determination? If so, you WILL find Him. Anything less and you'll find yourself deeply frustrated or disillusioned. Does this sound familiar? As you go through this study pray, **"Father God, I want to know You. Help me to seek You. Help me find You."**

How to do an FLQA Bible Study

1. Pray and ask God to teach you and show you what is true.
2. Read the verse and the surrounding chapter.
   Sample Verse: *"Be kind and compassionate to one another, forgiving each other, just as in Christ God forgave you"* (Eph. 4:32).
3. Write the facts from the verse in the column labeled "FACTS."

FACT	LESSON	QUESTION	ACTION
Be kind and compassionate to one another. Forgive each other. Forgive just as in Christ God forgave you.			

4. In the LESSON column, write out the lessons that the facts teach you. Do this for all the facts listed.

FACT	LESSON	QUESTION	ACTION
Be kind and compassionate to one another.	God tells me to be kind. He also tells me to be compassionate. I am to be kind and compassionate to other believers.		
Forgive each other.	We are to forgive each other. Forgiveness is the only option God gives me when I've been hurt by someone.		
Forgive just as in Christ God forgave you.	I am to forgive just as Jesus has me. I am not just to forgive in my own strength, but need God's help to completely forgive as He has me.		

5. In the QUESTION column, write questions to ask yourself based on each lesson point.

FACT	LESSON	QUESTION	ACTION
Be kind and compassionate to one another.	God tells me to be kind. He also tells me to be compassionate. I am to be kind and compassionate to other believers.	Who am I not kind to? Why? What prevents me from being kind? What attitude has replaced compassion in me? What Christians do I lack kindness and compassion for?	
Forgive each other.	We are to forgive each other. Forgiveness is the only option God gives me when I've been hurt by someone.	Who do I hold unforgiveness toward and for what? What was their offense I chose not to forgive? What have I chosen to do instead of forgive?	
Forgive just as in Christ God forgave you.	I am to forgive just as Jesus has me. I am not just to forgive in my own strength, but need God's help to completely forgive as He has me.	How did God forgive me in Christ? How has my attitude toward them fallen short of God's standards of forgiveness? Have I offered a lesser forgiveness? How?	

6. For the ACTION column, list actions you could put in place in your life based on the questions you just asked.

FACT	LESSON	QUESTION	ACTION
Be kind and compassionate to one another.	God tells me to be kind. He also tells me to be compassionate. I am to be kind and compassionate to other believers.	Who am I not kind to? Why? What prevents me from being kind? What attitude has replaced compassion in me? What Christians do I lack kindness and compassion for?	I will study selfishness with the goal of removing it! I will go to (insert name) and bless them. Apathy. I will **NOT** allow this attitude to remain. I will confess it, and leave it behind.
Forgive each other.	We are to forgive each other. Forgiveness is the only option God gives me when I've been hurt by someone.	Who do I hold unforgiveness toward and for what? What was their offense I chose not to forgive? What have I chosen to do instead of forgive?	I will go to (insert name) and apologize. I will forgive their rudeness and offense. I will pray for them. I will ignore them no more. I will not avoid them but will seek them out.
Forgive just as in Christ God forgave you.	I am to forgive just as Jesus has me. I am not just to forgive in my own strength, but need God's help to completely forgive as He has me.	How did God forgive me in Christ? How has my attitude toward them fallen short of God's standards of forgiveness? Have I offered a lesser forgiveness? How?	I will sacrifice my pride and say, "I am sorry." I will ask God to change my heart and give me total forgiveness for (insert name) until I possess it.

7. Pick at least one action step. Commit to follow through with it for a week. Journal your results.

How to Write a Heart Psalm

Honesty and Transparency. These are two essentials to praying but two things that many find difficult to express to God in words.

Heart Psalms are a simple tool to help you talk to God honestly and transparently and to express to God what is going on deep inside of your heart.

We encourage you to have a notebook or journal handy as you work through *First Love*. You many find you need more room than the pages provided to express your heart.

First, quiet yourself.

Next, think of a word that describes the condition of your heart before God. No need to rush!

When you have that word, write it at the top of the Heart Psalm page where it says:

"Lord, my heart before you today is_____(insert your word)_____."

Now—the KEY STEP—think of two word-pictures that describe the word you've come up with. Next, write those word-pictures in the two spaces provided after, "It is like a:"

Now, write your heart to God. Remember, you are writing to God, not journaling, not simply writing your thoughts. You are talking to and expressing yourself to a God who loves you! Pour out all the contents of your heart. Heart Psalms don't have to rhyme or be of any specific length. Just be **honest and transparent.**

Here is an example from a real person named Pippa!

Numb
Lord, my heart before you today is <u>numb.</u>

It is like: an ice cube held down on the skin for too long.

Lord my heart before You today is numb like an ice cube held down on the skin for too long, knowing that the numbness is only temporary and it will go away in time, but yet a true, current reality. Like the ice cube—someone has to hold it there to enable the skin to become numb. I know I am the reason for my own numb heart. I have pushed You to one side and tried to live life on my own again, thinking that I don't need You God. Yet now I'm turning to you KNOWING I need You Jesus, but so much has happened in the past year. I have tried to block out pain and grief—I HATE feeling hurt—who doesn't? But instead of coming to You I've tried to get through on my own. I've suppressed EVERYTHING and feel consumed by mess. I put that ice cube on my heart, because I was overwhelmed and was honestly just fed up with feeling, feeling grief, feeling alone, feeling selfish, feeling negative, feeling ANYTHING. It brought me back to the question that makes my mind and heart scream out WHY AM I HERE?

I've been wallowing in my own pool of numbness for too long. The other reason why I've put that ice cube on my skin/heart is because I'm scared of being in that right place with You. I'm scared of stepping out, scared of how You will fully use me, scared of standing out. Yet deep, deep down under the numbness of my heart it wants to jump for joy and see life in color again, it wants to be obedient, but right now it feels like it doesn't know You any more—the numbness has drowned out Your voice. Yet searching my numb heart, part of it doesn't believe that it deserves to be defrosted.

It is like: just having an anesthetic at the dentist and not being able to speak properly.

Lord, my heart is numb like a mouth that has just had an anesthetic at the dentist. There are words that want to come out, that want to communicate with You, but they're all just a jumbled mess and aren't coherent, so after a few feeble attempts I just can't be bothered. Listen to me! I have become LAZY. I have been distracted by trying to distract myself! Distracting myself from You, but also myself! I spend hours playing games online, scrolling through social media, or keeping myself busy with STUFF. I'll do anything not to talk to You; it's like an ongoing battle in my mind—a part of me knows/wants to talk to You or acknowledge my deep inner thoughts, the thought goes through my mind, and in a split second it's gone! I'm doing something else. And yet just like trying to take a drink with a numb mouth—it will all spill out one way or another when I'm not expecting it.

Lord I need to know You as my Father again, I need to know that You care about me and not just the things I try and do for You. I've heard all this Christian jargon for too long about Your "grace" and "mercy," and how there is nothing I can do to earn Your love or to make You love me more or less. But I don't KNOW it in my heart. Help me to get back to You. I need Your help, Lord.

LESSON 1

Why Do I Feel Unaccepted By God?

Scripture: John 14

Key Verses: John 14:23–24

> *"Jesus replied, 'Anyone who loves me will obey my teaching. My Father will love them, and we will come to them and make our home with them. Anyone who does not love me will not obey my teaching. These words you hear are not my own; they belong to the Father who sent me.'"*

After you have read all of John 14, take a minute and discuss the following.

Have you ever found or heard a common factor in those who argue against God's existence? Their point of contention can be traced back to a self-first motive. In other words they use themselves as a reference point, **not truth** (God's word). Take the end of a closed relationship for example. Many people can't reconcile God allowing that to happen, so it becomes easier to believe that there's no God or if there is, that He doesn't care. They are using themselves as the starting point to determine their beliefs about who God is or isn't. Can you see how a person could develop this kind of thinking? Have you?

In John 14 we see a clear truth: **you cannot love God and not care about His commandments**. Loving God and obeying Him are inseparable, which is the opposite of what we see in many people, churches, and religious activities.

When was the last time you heard something about God, and it was related to your sin? It is not popular to talk about sin, or what is right or wrong according to God. Instead we hear things like "Do what you think is best," "Follow your heart," or "You have to do what is right for you." Those statements are man-centered not God-centered. As you read John 14, it is clear what man's original sin was. It was that people concluded that they themselves, and not God, had the right to determine what was right and wrong for them. This is not a new idea; in fact it originated in the Garden of Eden. Man made a choice that regardless of all their needs and desires being provided for in the garden it was best for them to eat of the fruit God clearly had forbidden. Mankind discarded obedience, and as a result broke their relationship with God (Gen. 3:1–6).

This attitude has been in the heart of every person since then. Theologians call this the sinful nature of man. In the 1700s there was a king in Prussia named Frederick. One day he was visiting a prison in his country. He noticed that every inmate he talked to proclaimed, "I am innocent! I am innocent!" However just before he left the prison, he met one inmate who said this, "I deserve this punishment!" The king in response said, "Release this man. We wouldn't want this one guilty man to corrupt the whole prison filled with innocent men." With this, they released the prisoner who could admit his guilt. Seems a little contrary to our justice system, but this is true with God. God says in 1 John 1:9, **"If we confess our sin to Him He is faithful and just to forgive us of our sin and to cleanse us from all of unrighteousness."**

People may say they want a close relationship with God and will explore many means to get there. They may try meditation, yoga, horoscopes, drugs, cults, and any number of religions. However, the one thing that they don't consider is following God's way as outlined in the Bible.

If you were God, would you find it easy to have a relationship with people who

- dispute Your authority?
- question the moral boundaries You established?
- rewrite Your house rules?
- doubt Your character?
- claim equality with You?
- deny Your truth?
- accuse You of not caring?
- complain when they don't get their way?
- say You exist, but act like You don't?

Many people have adopted these attitudes, yet can't understand why they don't feel close to God and even go on to blame God for their lack of relationship. It comes across like the toddler who, when he gets punished, screams at of the top of his lungs, "I don't like you! You don't love me!"

Discussion Question: Go through the questions above. How have you been guilty of them?

There are many angry people and some who have gone numb, because they are tired of being frustrated in "trying God." This disappointment in God comes from a result of our own disrespect of Him and an unwillingness to obey His word. If you are angry or numb, can you understand that **the source of your pain is disillusionment with God?**

Remember the original question: why do I feel like I am unaccepted by God?

The most important reason that we feel unaccepted by God is the simple fact we have not been made right with Him and in our sinful state we are not acceptable. We don't feel accepted because we're not; we still stand rebellious and guilty before Him.

John 3:16–21 says:

"For God so loved the world that He gave His one and only Son, that whoever believes in Him shall not perish but have eternal life. For God did not send his Son into the world to condemn the world, but to save the world through him. Whoever believes in him is not condemned, but whoever does not believe

stands condemned already because they have not believed in the name of God's one and only Son. This is the verdict: Light has come into the world, but people loved darkness instead of light because their deeds were evil. Everyone who does evil hates the light, and will not come into the light for fear that their deeds will be exposed. But whoever lives by the truth comes into the light, so that it may be seen plainly that what they have done has been done in the sight of God."

Take a look at Genesis 3. Here's the picture:

An angel stands with a flaming sword at the gate of Eden. Reentrance into the garden for Adam and Eve has been denied. The door of access to God is slammed shut and sealed. Mankind stands outside God's presence for the first time, afraid, naked, lonely, guilty, and ashamed. They have now entered into a world where Satan's anger, hatred, and plans run free. The record even says Satan crouched outside their doors waiting to pounce on them (Gen. 4:7). But these fallen children of God are still loved, and His love would span any divide, pay any cost, even the cost of His own son's life (Jesus) to be reconciled with them. When a child is punished by his or her parent, the love for that child doesn't change. The same is so much truer with God.

This is where the Gospel of Jesus Christ is born. **The good news is that Jesus Christ came into the world to reopen the door** and once again grant access to God. Jesus was willing to die on a cross to pay the penalty for our disobedience, and therefore reconcile us with God. If you find the message of the Gospel frustrating, consider it frustrates those who falsely believe they can come to God on their own terms. Are you refusing to recognize it is your sin that shut the door of relationship with God in the first place, and it's your sin that keeps Him out? **Only Jesus can reopen that door. If we struggle with acceptance from God, it is because of us, not because of God.** There is nothing, no service, no good deed, no lifetime of kindness or generosity that can make us acceptable in God's eyes. It is only through the blood of Christ that God can look upon us and welcome us into His gates.

John 14:6 says: (Jesus speaking) *"I am the way and the truth and the life. No man comes to the Father except through me."*

The first step in having a close, deep, and passionate relationship with God starts with Him pointing out and disciplining us for our sin. *Hebrews 12:6 (NLT) says, "For the Lord disciplines those he loves, and he punishes each one he accepts as his child."* Sometimes we wonder why life seems so difficult, and God seems so distant. Is it possible that God needs to use extreme circumstances, tragedy, frustration, and difficulties to wake up our souls to the serious situation we are in?

'Fess Up

- **Am I angry or numb toward God? Why?**

- Have I ever recognized that the distance between me and God is because of my sin, not because of anything He has done?

- What specific moments in my life have made me feel unaccepted by God?

FLQA

"Jesus replied, 'Anyone who loves me will obey my teaching. My Father will love them, and we will come to them and make our home with them. Anyone who does not love me will not obey my teaching. These words you hear are not my own; they belong to the Father who sent me.'"

John 14:23-24

FACT	LESSON	QUESTION	ACTION

Pick an ACTION step to carry out this week and DO IT!

Key Question
What unresolved feelings do I have toward God?

SOLITUDE. Spend five minutes quieting your heart and listening to God. Write here what He said:

Heart Psalm

Father, my heart before you today is:_____

It is like:

It is like:

Prayer for the Week

"God, reveal truth to me. Help me see You. Show me where I have been disobedient. Open the door of my heart, and come in. Use my questions and difficulties, and show Yourself to me through them. I want to love You, and I know that begins with obedience. Help me to obey You and Your word. In Jesus's name, Amen."

LESSON 2

Who is God?

Scripture: John 3:16–21

Key Verse: John 3:16

"For God so loved the world that He gave His one and only Son, that whoever believes in Him shall not perish but have eternal life."

If you are to know and understand God, you must start with the concept of His complete "otherness." It simply means that God cannot be comprehended. He is distinct from anything and everything we know. If he wasn't He could not be God. We cannot even fully imagine Him because anything we could create in our minds must fall short of who He is. If not, then he could not have created us. Nothing can be created by something that is lesser than them. No computer can build a program without a human. No car can repair or improve itself. The Creator, who is greater than His creation is the only one. This is a difficult truth to surrender to. A. W. Tozer once said, "We want a God we can in some measure control. We need the feeling of security that comes from knowing what God is like, and what He is like is of course a composite of all the religious pictures we have seen, all the best people we have known or heard about, and all sublime ideas we have entertained" (*The Knowledge of the Holy*, 6). God is and has to be greater than us. Without this realization you can never enter into a whole relationship with Him. I once heard an atheist say, "The reason I'm an atheist is primarily because I cannot come up with a version of God that I can understand." That person is on a futile journey, because God by definition cannot be understood. In Psalm 8:1–4 it says:

"O Lord, our Lord, how majestic is Your name in all the earth! You have set your glory above the heavens. From the lips of children and infants you have ordained praise because of your enemies, to silence the foe and the avenger. When I consider your heavens, the work of your fingers, the moon and the stars, which you have set in place, what is man that you are mindful of him, the son of man that you care for him?"

Without an understanding of the "otherness" of God, we would have no reason to worship Him. He must be greater than us to be due praise. If God were not incomprehensible there would be no need for faith and our life would be filled with questions which no one greater could answer. Why would you submit to, or worship, your equal?

This is why for many people religion becomes stale so quickly. The beauty of the Bible is that God has revealed Himself to us through it. The Bible is full of characteristics about God that allow us to know Him in His love, His might, His holiness, His plan for us. Jesus makes this "otherness" completely knowable and enables us to be in relationship with him. John 1:14 says: *"The Word became flesh and made his dwelling among us. We have seen His glory, the glory of the one and only Son, who came from the Father, full of grace and truth."*

There are basically four relationships that we have with God:

First—He is **our MASTER,** and we are His servants. Our duty is to **OBEY.**
Second—He is a **FRIEND,** so we are His friends. This demands **LOYALTY.**
Third—He is **our LOVER,** so we are His. This requires **FAITHFULNESS.**
Fourth—He is **our FATHER,** so we are His children. This requires **RESPECT.**

The primary relationship we need to focus on is God as Father.

Discussion Question: Do I want God to be my Father? Why or why not?

We have become disconnected from God, our Master, our Friend, our Lover, and most importantly our Father. **Our disobedience** to His Word, the Bible has distanced us from God. **Our lack of loyalty** to Him as our friend has separated us from Him. **Our unfaithfulness** to God, in loving so many things more than Him, has divorced us from Him.

Our lack of respect for Him and His Word is the reason we feel so distant from Him. This is the condition of all people everywhere. Everyone is alienated from God because of sin. Romans 3:23 says it this way…*"For all have sinned and fall short of the glory of God."*

Key Point: If we are not close to God as father, it is because of our sin of disobedience, our lack of loyalty to Him, our having other gods before Him, and our continual disrespect for His word and Him as a father.

Discussion Question: Why is it that many people have no relationship with God?

'Fess Up

- **Do I obey God as Master?**

- **Am I loyal to Him as a friend?**

- **Do I love Him by keeping Him first?**

- **Do I respect Him as my Father by keeping His word?**

- **How did it go with the action steps this last week?**

FLQA

"For God so loved the world that He gave His only son that whoever believes in Him should not perish but have eternal life."

John 3:16

FACT	LESSON	QUESTION	ACTION

Pick an ACTION step to carry out this week and DO IT!

Key Question
Who is God?

SOLITUDE. Spend five minutes quieting your heart and listening to God. Write here what He said:

Heart Psalm

Father, my heart before you today is:_____

It is like:

It is like:

Prayer for the Week

"Father God, I love You, help me love You more. Show me how to be a loyal friend to You. Help me put You first in everything. Show me what a good father You are. I want to know You better. In Jesus's name, Amen."

LESSON 3

Who Am I?

Scripture: Genesis 2:4–25

Key Verse: Genesis 2:7

"...the Lord God formed the man from the dust of the ground and breathed into his nostrils the breath of life, and the man became a living being."

C S Lewis once said, *"You do not have a soul. You are a soul. You have a body."* Having a proper perspective of who you are and what makes up your life, is one of the most important things you'll ever spend time thinking about. The Bible makes it clear that your body is important; however your soul is much more important. **You are your soul.** Matthew 16:26 says, *"What good will it be for someone to gain the whole world, yet forfeit their souls? Or what can anyone give in exchange for their soul?"* Why is our soul so important? Our soul will last for eternity, our bodies will not. Unfortunately, this is a difficult perspective to maintain on a daily basis. Our bodies require great attention, our thoughts are naturally centered on eating, sleeping, cleaning, exercising—things we need daily. It is easier to think of these things because of the here and now rather than taking care of our unseen soul. If we give all this attention to our body which is only here for a little while, how much more attention should we give to our soul which will live on forever? In fact, for too many of us the body has replaced the soul as the most important part of who we are (i.e., how we look, what we spend our time and money). **God understands the value of our soul,** which is why He is always trying to get our attention and remind us of it.

Discuss the following questions:

- Either God created man or He didn't. What impact does your decision have on your other beliefs about God?
- What would be the motive for mankind to try to disprove or discredit God as Creator?

If you remove God from the equation, man has no one that he has to answer to, except himself. (Isn't that convenient?) He then becomes top dog.

Genesis tells us that man wanted to live with God in the garden, but he wanted to live there without the boundaries set up by a loving, holy, and pure God. The same is true today.

Discussion Question: Has this thinking affected you? How?

The soul is the spiritual part of you. According to the Bible, without believing in God as Creator, you believe you are just a body without a soul.

If there is no God, then there's no spiritual dynamic. If you believe there is no soul, then you believe there is nothing after this life. Therefore, the only thing that has value in this life is getting all you can out of it. This breeds selfishness. Selfishness then determines your morals, values, and urges. This thinking has even invaded many religious people's theology (view of God).

Also, when you believe there is no soul or God, this eliminates all hope. There are many people today who claim that God does not exist. But could it be that those who make such a claim may have known of God at one point, but choose to walk away from God because they disagree with Him? Specifically because they disagreed on how they wanted to live their life as compared to how God wanted them to live their life. They may also walk away, because they want no one to answer to.

Often well-meaning seekers of God and people-focused ministries can complicate things. They spend much time, energy, and money trying to meet the needs of the body and its appetites, while downplaying God's truth and standards that have been established for the benefit of the soul.

Modern society is no place to look for opinions on God, because our culture is saturated with people who want to rule themselves. They believe life happened by chance. They will cry that we should act "humanely" toward each other, but at the same time they will attend a protest against God, declaring we are nothing more than evolved beasts.

Once you remove God, two groups of people will fight to take His place:

Megalomaniacs—those who want to rule the world
Erotimaniacs—those who want to indulge in the world

Discussion Questions: What happens when the ones in charge of our society, view themselves as bodies with little or no emphasis on their souls? What will they prioritize? What will they do away with?

Just a few months ago I did the funeral for my wife's mother. She was in her eighties. She died from complications of Alzheimer's. She had been married to my wife's dad, for over sixty years. Yet, on the day of her funeral we celebrated. Why? Because we know where her soul is. It is in heaven! I shared II Corinthians 5:8 which says, *"To be absent from the body is to be present with the Lord."* I told everyone present that *she* was not the one absent, *we* were. From God's perspective *our souls* are the absent ones. Our souls are the ones separated from their Creator, and God's perspective is ALWAYS more important than ours.

In Mark 8, Jesus asks two very significant questions that all of us must answer:

"What does it profit a man if he gains the whole world but loses his soul?"
"What will a man give in exchange for his soul?"

Is it possible that many of people's problems and inability to connect with God, stem from the fact that they are so focused on their bodies, their lusts, their urges, seeking pleasure, and ruling their own lives, that they have totally neglected their souls. God's primary concern and the part of our being He relates to is our soul. To walk closer to God we must give our souls more attention than our bodies. This is the purpose of the exercises in this book!

    Discussion Questions: Can you name a few people who have walked away from church, God, religion, and faith over this very issue? Do you wrestle with this?

'Fess Up

- **You say you want to have a relationship with God, but how are you seeking to do it on your own terms? Isn't that just what Adam and Eve did?**

- **In what ways do you struggle to have faith in God because:**
  1. **You want to rule your own life?**

  2. **You want to indulge yourself in things to which God has said "no"?**

  3. **You care more about your body than you do your soul?**

- **How did it go with the action steps this last week?**

FLQA

"...the Lord God formed the man from the dust of the ground and breathed into his nostrils the breath of life, and the man became a living being."

Genesis 2:7

FACT	LESSON	QUESTION	ACTION

Pick an ACTION step to carry out this week and DO IT!

Key Questions

What would it look like in my life to prioritize my body over my soul?

What would it look like in my life to prioritize my soul over my body?

SOLITUDE. Spend five minutes quieting your heart and listening to God. Write here what He said:

Heart Psalm

Father, my heart before you today is:_____

It is like:

It is like:

Prayer for the Week

"Father, I believe You created my soul and my body. I'm asking You to help me know You better. Show me who You are, so I can give my life over to Your rule. Teach me to obey Your Word and not indulge in things that You have forbidden that hurt me. Help me to care more about the condition of my soul. In Jesus's name, Amen."

LESSON 4

Why Do I Feel Like I've Missed God?

Scripture: John 6:25–40

Key Verse: John 6:35

"Then Jesus declared, 'I am the bread of life. Whoever comes to me will never go hungry and whoever believes in me will never be thirsty.'"

Have you ever gone to a Christian gathering hoping to find a personal experience with God, yet walked away feeling like you missed God entirely?

One Sunday I grabbed my seat in the back of the sanctuary. As the music played, I found it incredibly repetitive. It was so distorted by the volume pushed through an overextended sound system. On this morning I so desperately wanted to hear from Jesus. As I sat there, over and over again this phrase resounded, "I need more of you, I need more of you, I need more of you…"

The lyrics then shifted to a long set of, "I am hungry for you, I am hungry for you, I am hungry for you…"

This truly was the cry of my heart. **I was starving, and wondered would I see Him, meet Him, hear from Him, and get to know Him?** As I sat through the service, it contained no Scripture, no clear message, no quiet, no waiting on Him. There seemed to be very little room for Him to speak. So when I thought no one was watching, I slipped out.

As I went outside, I wanted to seek after Jesus. I walked across the street, where a man was remodeling his house. He appeared stern. He was unresponsive to my words of greeting and even seemed bothered by them. His music was blaring too, pushing its speaker's limit, trying to compete with the clamor coming from the sanctuary. It too was distorted in both melody and in lyrics, much like what I had just run from. The lyrics were eerily similar to the chants of the church. The singer mused, "I am lonely, I am lonely, I am lonely." Then went into the refrain, "I am hungry, I am hungry, I am hungry…for your sweet smile."

As I stood there, I realized the church and the world were singing the same sad song, using repetition and volume to combat loneliness and the ache of the absence of someone they loved. In both situations the music may have soothed for a moment, but in the long run it just made the pain deeper. I asked myself what was the point of repetitively singing how thirsty or hungry we were for God? I thought of how much we need Jesus's presence, yet we are refusing to be quiet and wait for Him. **How can we expect Him to show up if we leave**

out His word, the Bible from our gatherings? How do we expect to have meaningful times with Him when our prayers are short and short lived?

In my loneliness, I sat between the two sets of blaring music. A picture came to my mind of a person battling anorexia, someone who is starving in hopes of having happiness, fulfillment, and love but can never know those things in their entirety because of the pain from the emptiness inside. If we say we want to hear from God, to know Him, to meet with Him, but are like people anxious with food, we cannot know satisfaction. We must slow down enough and wait for Him to feed us. Nibbling at God's truth and constantly repeating how famished we are, has replaced dining on Jesus, God's spiritual bread. Only sipping has kept us from quenching our thirst. **We can drink from His Living water, His holy presence, and thirst no more**. He has a feast for us—His Word. We can be filled by the meat of God which our souls long for. I ended that morning grieving and praying for the singers, both secular and religious. My heart craved a song in and about the very presence of Jesus.

A number of years ago, I was very ill. I was plagued by chronic dizziness, sleeplessness, and anxiety. After months of this, I felt like I was going crazy. I thought some rest would help and flew down to Florida to find some, but found none. One night around 2:00 a.m., I was walking down the beach. I was angry and frustrated with God. I stooped down and picked up a starfish. I held it up in the sky and yelled at God, "Don't you care about me? I care more for this starfish than you do for me!" I walked about another quarter mile down the beach, where I stopped again, bent down, and picked up a handful of sand.

Again I held it up to the sky with tears in my eyes crying and said, "God don't you see me? Am I no more important to you than these grains of sand? Where are you God? Speak to me!" With that I heard in my spirit, "Look down." I looked down and noticed that I was standing in the middle of a circle. But it wasn't a circle; it was the letter O. As I took some steps back, I could see that someone had written something in the sand. They had written "AWESOME GOD," and I had been standing in the very center of GOD. I cried. I felt so loved. God arranged all those circumstances to show me He was with me and loved me.

Matthew 6:25–33 reminds us of Jesus's words, *"Therefore I tell you, do not worry about your life, what you will eat or drink; or about your body, what you will wear. Is not life more than food, and the body more than clothes? Look at the birds of the air; they do not sow or reap or store away in barns, and yet your heavenly Father feeds them. Are you not much more valuable than they? Can any one of you by worrying add a single hour to your life? And why do you worry about clothes? See how the flowers of the field grow. They do not labor or spin. Yet I tell you that even Solomon in all his splendor was not dressed like one of these. If that is how God clothes the grass of the field, which is here today and tomorrow is thrown into the fire, will he not much more clothe you—you of little faith? So do not worry, saying, 'What shall we eat?' or 'What shall we drink?' or 'What shall we wear?'"*

God sees you. He cares for you. He will be found if you search for Him with all your heart.

'Fess Up

- **Do you seek God? How?**

- **Are you trying to fill your God-sized hole without Him?**

- **Is your attempt at a "God fix" leaving you starving for more?**

FLQA

"Jesus declared, "I am the bread of life. Whoever comes to me will never go hungry and he who believes in me will never be thirsty.'"

John 6:35

FACT	LESSON	QUESTION	ACTION

Pick an ACTION step to carry out this week and DO IT!

Key Question
Why do I feel so empty inside even though I do "religious things?"

SOLITUDE. Spend five minutes quieting your heart and listening to God. Write here what He said:

Heart Psalm

Father, my heart before you today is:_____

It is like:

 It is like:

Prayer for the Week

"Father, draw me into Your presence. Meet with me today. Feed my soul. Help me know Your love. Help me see You in my life and all around me. Assist me in understanding Your word. I pray this in Jesus's name, Amen."

LESSON 5

Why Don't I Know The Love of A Heavenly Father?

Scripture: Romans 8:13–17

Key Verse: Romans 8:15

"The Spirit you received does not make you slaves, so that you live in fear again; rather, the Spirit you received brought about your adoption to sonship. And by him we cry, 'Abba, Father.'"

If you read the Bible from beginning to end, you will see that its basic story is about a Father who loves His children very much. **The Bible is story after story of people, who through their disobedience have broken off the relationship God wants to have with them.**

The Bible makes it very clear that the reason people don't know or sense God's love for them is because of their own sin. Disrespect, selfishness, and rebellion toward Him are symptoms.

When I first met Woody (not his real name), he was twelve years old. He lived in a small town and had a very poor family life. His stepfather was particularly mean and uncaring. He often reminded Woody that he was not his father; he did not have a father and never would.

Can you imagine what this did to the heart of this little boy? This was his only experience with a father figure. Are your images of God muddied by your experiences?

Today Woody is an adult in his forties. He has a broken marriage, jealousy issues, and severed relationships with his family. He has no relationship at all with his mom. He is a people pleaser in an effort to earn acceptance from both people and God. Recently he said to me about his relationship with God, "I tried as hard as I could to make God happy…but I never succeeded." You see, Woody had a misconception of what a father should be. His poor earthly representation of God the Father hindered his capacity to see God as a loving father.

Discussion Question: What are the characteristics of a great father?

God is all these things and more. Psalm 68:5–6 says that God is "A father to the fatherless…God sets the lonely in families, he leads forth the prisoners with singing…"

Once we see, believe, and understand that **God is a good and loving father,** and we admit we have been selfish, cowardly, and rebellious (sinners), we can have hope of reconciliation with Him. We can experience and be fulfilled by the love of our Heavenly Father regardless of what kind of dad we had or didn't have on earth.

'Fess Up

- **Do you know and trust God as a good and loving Father? Why or why not?**

- **How did it go with the action steps this last week?**

FLQA

"The Spirit you received does not make you slaves, so that you live in fear again;
Rather, the Spirit you received brought about your adoption to sonship. And by him we cry, "Abba, Father."
Romans 8:15

FACT	LESSON	QUESTION	ACTION
			Pick an ACTION step to carry out this week and DO IT!

Key Question
Why don't I sense God's presence or His love?

SOLITUDE. Spend five minutes quieting your heart and listening to God. Write here what He said:

Heart Psalm

Father, my heart before you today is:_____

It is like:

It is like:

Prayer for the Week

"God, I believe You love me and want to be with me! Show yourself to me. Amen."

LESSON 6

Who Has the Right to Determine Right and Wrong and Why?

Scripture: 1 John 1:5–10, 1 John 2:3–6

Key Verses: 1 John 1:8–10

"If we claim to be without sin, we deceive ourselves, and the truth is not in us. If we confess our sins, He is faithful and just and will forgive us our sins and purify us from all unrighteousness. If we claim we have not sinned, we make Him out to be a liar, and His word has no place in our lives."

Having the right perspective on God and His Law is essential. Where do our laws come from? What dictates what we do with our lives as either right or wrong? We are taught about man's law at a very young age from stealing, cheating, speeding, to murder, and so on. But where do these laws originate? And why are some of them the same as or just like the Ten Commandments in the Bible? Could it be that the God who created man instilled in him what we often refer to as our conscience, the nagging feeling that something is wrong? The purpose of the Ten Commandments was not for us to be able to prove how good we can be. Rather, it was to show us how naturally disobedient to God we are. Knowing God's law and how far from it our hearts are shows us a destroyed and separated relationship with God. Galatians 3:14 says, *"Why, then, was the law given at all? It was added because of transgressions until the Seed to whom the promise referred had come."* It was given to show people their sin and how we can never, on our own, live up to God's standard.

Without the Law of God, we would never know that we have broken it. Without the Law of God, we make up our own ideas for knowing or pleasing God. When we do this, we usually come up with laws bent toward our advantage, making God's law devalued.

Greek mythology tells a tale of a man named Procrustes whose name meant "He who stretches." He kept a house by the side of the road, where he would offer to passing strangers a place to stay. He would invite them in for a meal and a night's rest in his very unique bed. He claimed it would automatically adjust to the height of whoever laid in it. Procrustes was an evil man, and what he didn't tell them was that as soon as they lay down on the bed, it would stretch them if they were too short, or cut off their legs if they were too tall. Eventually the tables were turned on Procrustes, and he met his fate upon that very bed.

Like Procrustes, when we take God's law and try to make it fit our own end, we will die en route. When we "cut off" God's law, or try to stretch it to give us permission to do what we want, it ends up killing our souls. **The Bible tells us that God is both loving and just.** Psalms 145:7 (NLT) says: *"The Lord is righteous in everything He does; He's filled with kindness."* He is both love and truth. Take a minute to discuss how you feel about the following statement: **We live in a spiritual culture that worships God's attribute of love, but are consciously ignorant that He is equally truth. You cannot want God if you don't want truth too!**

Imagine someone charged with murder, and they are standing in front of a judge who is both loving and fair. What would you think of this defendant if they stated any of the following explanations for their actions?

- "I didn't like the law that forbids murder."
- "I don't understand the law that forbids murder."
- "Other people murder."
- "Judge, in enforcing this law you are unloving."
- "I don't agree with the law."
- "I interpret the law differently than you do."
- "The law is for criminals, not me."
- "I've always had a tendency to want to murder."

Now imagine you were the judge, and this murderer was someone you loved, a sibling, a child, a parent, or a best friend. What would you do? How would you feel? Though your heart may swell with compassion and kindness toward them, would you not rule according to the law? We can only see in a limited understanding of both love and justice. This is NOT true of God. God is not 50 percent love and 50 percent holy, and whatever the situation or person merits is the ruling force, but rather He is 100 percent love and 100 percent holy. One cannot overrule the other. He is both, completely, at all times. Understanding this takes faith as it is something we do not know in ourselves and therefore is hard to imagine. We choose to show either love or justice. **God is kind, but He is not soft.**

We are all guilty of constantly breaking God's law and there are no acceptable excuses. It is easy to think, "Well, I rarely do anything wrong," or "I don't do all the big sins." James 2:10 clearly says, "For whoever keeps the whole law and stumbles at JUST ONE POINT is guilty of breaking all of it." Change your perspective. Are you able to keep this standard? We all stand before God to be judged as guilty. But the good news is that Jesus Christ died to meet the requirements of the law that we could not.

In church we all learned that Jesus had to die on the cross to forgive our sins. But a key element to understand is that He had to live a *sinless, perfect life, keeping perfectly and completely God's law*. In doing this, He met God's requirement of keeping His law for us. This is the good news of the Bible! Now when we stand before God to be judged, Christ stands next to us as our lawyer and says to God the Father, "This one is with me." God sees Christ's blood that was shed, His payment, and not our sins against Him.

Jesus lived as a man and kept His father's law perfectly. Therefore, He was a worthy sacrifice in our place, to take the penalty for our lawbreaking, which is death. Romans 6:23 says, *"For the wages of sin is death, but the free gift of God is eternal life in Christ Jesus our Lord."* But without the law outlined by God, we would never know our need or our guilt or our impending punishment. **God gave the law because of His great love for us.**

Romans 8:1–4 says, *"Therefore, there is now no condemnation for those who are in Christ Jesus, because through Christ Jesus the law of the Spirit of life set me free from the law of sin and death. For what the law was powerless to do in that it was weakened by the sinful nature, God did by sending His own Son in the likeness of sinful man to be a sin offering. And so He condemned sin in sinful man, in order that the righteous requirements of the law might be fully met in us, who do not live according to the sinful nature but according to the Spirit."*

The point? Until you admit you are a lawbreaker and recognize you are guilty before God, you cannot become a Christian. It isn't until you hate your lawbreaking sin just like God does and confess your guilt to God that He can forgive you. The Law of God (summarized in the Ten Commandments) tells us what is required by God to be right with Him. A sinful nature makes this impossible. Romans 3:23 says, *"…for all have sinned and fall short of the glory of God."*

There was a young girl who time and time again prayed to have a relationship with God. Six times she asked God to come into her life. Yet every time she went back to all the empty and sinful things she had been doing. She wanted to know God, but felt guilty and condemned all the time. She went to her youth pastor and said, "What's wrong with me?" He said to her, "First, stop praying that prayer. Let's not repeat what isn't working." He said, "Talk to God. Picture yourself standing before Him as your judge. Think about the reality of hell and death. Cry out, 'I am guilty of breaking your law. Please forgive me. Save me from the punishment I deserve. Save me Jesus, and please help me from now on to love You and obey You.'" She immediately broke down crying, realizing what was missing. She finally saw how her sin had hurt God. She sincerely confessed her sin and asked God to make her into a new person. She went back the next night and told her youth pastor. "The love and forgiveness of God is so real to me now, that if every person in the world lined up to convince me that it wasn't true, it wouldn't shake my confidence at all." Today she loves and knows her God.

'Fess Up

- **How have I edited the following laws?**
  - **You shall have no other gods before me.**

  - **You shall not misuse the name of the Lord your God.**

  - **Remember the Sabbath day by keeping it holy.**

- **How did it go with the action step from this last week?**

FLQA

"If we claim to be without sin, we deceive ourselves and the truth is not in us. If we confess our sins, He is faithful and just and will forgive us our sins and purify us from all unrighteousness. If we claim we have not sinned, we make Him out to be a liar and His word has no place in our lives.
I John 1:8–10

FACT	LESSON	QUESTION	ACTION

Pick an ACTION step to carry out this week and DO IT!

Key Question
Who has the right to determine what is right and wrong and why?

SOLITUDE. Spend five minutes quieting your heart and listening to God. Write here what He said:

Heart Psalm

Father, my heart before you today is:_____

It is like:

It is like:

Prayer for the Week

"Father, I realize Your commandments are for my good. I ask that You use Your commandments to show me where I have disobeyed You, and give me the humble heart I need to submit to them. Thank You for giving Jesus Christ, who paid the penalty for my disobedience by dying on the cross."

LESSON 7

Why Does Jesus Seem Harsh and Exclude So Many People?

Scripture: John 14: 1–14

Key Verse: John 14:6

"Jesus answered, 'I am the way and the truth and the life. No one comes to the Father except through me.'"

The claims of Jesus Christ are shocking. They were to the people who lived while He walked the earth, and they still are today. The claims He makes bother most atheists, agnostics, humanists, religious leaders, and surprisingly the majority of people who fill the pews in Christian churches.
Here are some of Jesus's claims about Himself:

- John 14:6—I am the **only way** to God. There is no other way.
- John 3:3—Unless you allow Me to radically transform your life you will never make it to heaven or have a relationship with God.

  In John 3, we read (paraphrasing) of a man Jesus met named Nick, a lifelong churchgoer and leader. Nick was very complimentary of Jesus. He said to Jesus, *"You seem like you know God."* Jesus responded, *"Well, it seems like you don't."* This upset Nick. He said, *"I know God. I'm sincere, I work hard at being good, am respected at church and I am part of God's approved group."* But Jesus knew his heart; his religion was unfulfilling. He felt condemnation, his spiritual life was lifeless, he had no joy and his many prayers never seemed to go beyond the ceiling. Sound familiar? He said, *"You cannot know God, unless I radically change your life."* Jesus put it this way, *"You must be born again."* Jesus said, *"I have no peers."* Jesus is not one of the many ways to approach God. He is not a pathway. He says, "I am the ONLY way."

- John 18:37—Everyone who sides with me, sides with the truth. If you side with someone else, anyone else, you side with liars.
- John 8:46, **He claimed He was sinless** and stated that He had never once broken any of God's laws. This was greatly difficult for the religious leaders of his time to accept. In fact many would pour their life's energy into proving He was a sinner by healing on the Sabbath.
- Luke 10:16 Jesus says that if you reject what He says, you reject God, the one who sent Him.

What Jesus said is true. Our opinion or level of understanding doesn't change that.

Suppose you found out that you had a tumor, and it is going to kill you. However you can be saved with major surgery. You may not like it, you may find it hard to accept, scary, unfamiliar, but that does not change the fact that the surgery is the only way for you to get better. We may want something more convenient, cheaper, easier, less painful; we may not even agree with the doctor's diagnosis, but that doesn't change the truth. Jesus may seem harsh or only available to some, because He is the only way. It is only through Him one can know God, be saved, and granted eternal life. His very nature, who He is, is exclusive. You must be a part of His family to not feel like an outsider.

In England I met a teenager named Ewan. He was going around sharing with anyone he could find, all of his perceived inconsistencies in the Bible. He had a computer printout of papers as thick as a phonebook. After about an hour, he worked his way over to me. I answered a great number of his questions, but he was relentless. So finally I said, "Ewan, I can prove to you that God exists, if you will answer one question for me." With that, he started to ask me another question. I was patient and answered the question, but as he went on to another question, I stopped him and made him listen. My question was this, "Ewan, do you love me?" He was taken back. He said "Noooooooo!" He said, "How does that prove that God exists?" I said, "Well, I love you and you are one of the rudest and most obnoxious people I've ever met. The reason I can love you is because I have God's love in my heart. The reason you don't love me is the absence of God in your life." He started to ask another question, I said, "Ewan, how can you resolve this?" He walked away. Ewan found himself outside of God's family and therefore didn't understand the ways, claims, or promises of Jesus. The "errors" he found in the Bible were in fact not God's errors or inconsistencies, but rather Ewan's error in not understanding. In asking about love he was thrown because he didn't understand that being a Christian was about having a relationship with God through Jesus, not another religion.

Jesus says, "*I am the way, the truth, and the life. No one comes unto the Father, but by Me*" (John 14:6).

Discussion Question: Based on what you just read, what separates Jesus from everyone else?

Key Point: Jesus alone resolved the problem we created by being breakers of God's law. Somebody guiltless had to pay a penalty of sin. He was the only one qualified, because He had never broken God's Law. He took care of our sin problem.

No one else can deal with your sin and the guilt you have before God, but in an attempt to do so religion takes sin and tries to

- explain it away,
- deny it,
- say it's not an issue with God,
- redefine it,
- convince people they have evolved past it,
- ignore it or just do the best you can because that's all God expects.

Do these sound familiar? Are they part of your thoughts and how you view God? Are you attempting an "easier" path to get to God? Without listening to what His son Jesus said, "*I do not set aside God's grace, for if righteousness could be gained through the law, Christ died for nothing*" (Gal. 2:21)!

'Fess Up

- **How do Jesus's claims of sinlessness make someone who is rebellious toward God feel?**

- **Why doesn't Jesus being the only way to God fit in with our tolerant society?**

- **How do you react when someone tells you, you MUST do something?**

- **How did it go with the action step from last week?**

FLQA

"Jesus answered, 'I am the way and the truth and the life. No one comes to the Father except through me.'"

John 14:6

FACT	LESSON	QUESTION	ACTION

Pick an **ACTION** step to carry out this week and **DO IT!**

Key Question
Why does Jesus seem harsh and exclude so many people?

SOLITUDE. Spend five minutes quieting your heart and listening to God. Write here what He said:

Heart Psalm

Father, my heart before you today is:_____

It is like:

It is like:

Prayer for the Week

*"Father, teach me to be willing to accept and understand Your way of salvation.
Help me put Your truth above any person's views or opinions, including my own.
I pray in the name of Your only son, Jesus."*

LESSON 8

How Could A Loving God Allow His Son to be Brutally Killed?

Scripture: Colossians 1:15–20

Key Verses: Colossians 1:15

"The Son is the image of the invisible God, the firstborn over all creation."

In Jesus Christ, God took on a face. That's what is meant in Colossians 1:15 when it says, *"The Son is the image of the invisible God."* Simply put, when you look at Jesus you're looking at God. Also see Hebrews 1:1–4 where Jesus is called, "the radiance of God's glory and the exact representation of his being…"

Today you generally find that people don't have a problem with the image of the "nice" Jesus. Many see Him as an important historical figure, a great teacher, or a religious leader. It's easy to like Him when you start dropping out some of the truths He taught. **We tend to conveniently discard or edit the words of Jesus we have problem with.** It is this that keeps Him at an arm's length preventing us from truly knowing Him.

But when we tinker with Jesus's word or conclude by consensus on a definition of Jesus that differs from the Bible, it is no longer an accurate portrait. It is now nothing more than a mirror that reflects us more than Him. It gives us a Jesus we think we can manage; a pocket-sized Jesus we can take out when convenient.

So there are many who feel they need to paint a new portrait of what Jesus looks like, to give Him a new and improved face. They keep some of the Bible's portrait, but add some personal preferences. How do they do this?

- They give new definitions to words He used. For example, the Bible tells us several times to FLEE from sin, but somehow we translate that as hang out awhile and try to resist it.
- They omit some of Jesus's teaching.
- They come up with new explanations of what Jesus really meant. Matthew 6:15 could be an example of the last point, and this one! It says, "But if you do not forgive others their sins, your Father will not forgive your sins." We think, "Surely, He means something else."
- They claim they have some new special insights on Jesus from God. We must be on our guard. God will NEVER contradict His word, and His word is NOT outdated or irrelevant.

Sometimes this inaccurate portrait of God is intentional, and sometimes it's out of a misunderstanding or naiveté. In either case the only way to correct this image of God is to go back to the most accurate source: the Bible.

When we get to heaven, God's probably not going to be upset that we didn't understand some of the obscure things in the Bible. What He will be upset with is when He clearly stated something and we refused to believe it.

Second Peter 1:19–20 says the only reliable resource we have is God's Word. *"And we have the word of the prophets made more certain, and you will do well to pay attention to it, as to a light shining in a dark place, until the day dawns and the morning star rises in your hearts. Above all, you must understand that no prophecy of Scripture came about by the prophet's own interpretation. For prophecy never had its origin in the will of man, but men spoke from God as they were carried along by the Holy Spirit."* It also says in John 1:1, "In the beginning was the Word, and the Word was with God and the Word was God." **God and His Word are inseparable.**

Discussion Question: How have I tried to separate God from His Word?

My brother Mike is an artist. He once was commissioned to paint a portrait of a very famous model. I walked into his studio one day to find him sitting there quietly not painting. I said, "Mike, what's wrong?" He answered, "Brad, I have painted many faces before, but this one I have to get just right; after all she is one the most famous faces in the world." He agonized because he wanted to get it right. Should we not exercise the same scrutiny when it comes to getting the portrait of Jesus accurate?

People like the "nice" Jesus...the Jesus of the Bible upsets them. He always has, always will. He speaks the truth, pulls no punches, yet at the same time He speaks with incredible love. Sometimes when you love someone you have to speak the truth they won't want to hear, even if you don't want to. I once had a friend who was on staff at a church. He confided in me that another pastor at that church was addicted to pornography, but no one knew. As hard as it was I gave him two options: you tell the leadership or I will. It was hard, but it was necessary. He chose to tell the leadership, and that pastor got the help he needed and was restored.

Though it was painful, wouldn't it have been wrong for me to allow this to go on? This could have impacted the whole church!

These are some of Jesus's hard truths:

- All men are sinners and have broken God's law (Rom. 3:23).
- The penalty for breaking God's law is death and hell (Rom. 6:23).
- No matter how good you are, you can never earn His favor (Eph. 2:9).
- The only way to deal with sin is to ask God for forgiveness (Acts 4:12).
- I am the only way to God (John 14:6).

If you remove these truths from the Bible, you are left with very little but nice feelings and inspirational stories. Many churches and Christians who remove Jesus's hard truth find that they must come up with alternatives to truth to attract people. Without God's love, truth, and power, they are forced to find other things to attract people. Crowds attract people, shows attract people, comfort attracts people, celebrities attract people, miracles attract people, food attracts people, and concerts attract people. They use attraction to attract people, but without the truth of Christ they eventually find these things empty and unfulfilling, and produce a culture of churchgoers who never truly know Christ.

I was once a guest speaker at a large youth event. In between sessions I went back to my room to rest and fell asleep. I had a dream: I was in a large auditorium and in the front stood a speaker. He was just a silhouette. Behind him I could see this little piece of wood sticking out. Eventually I could tell it was a cross, but could only see little pieces of it. Then I got a glimpse of the audience. It was thousands of sheep. Their eyes were bulging, and their tongues were hanging out. In the speaker's hand was an eyedropper and with it he was dropping little beads of water on their tongues, giving them just enough water to keep them coming back for more.

That's what happens in many places where people come out to hear about Jesus and His teaching. Speakers do nothing more than tease people into thinking they can have a relationship with God, but they fail to show them the way, leaving them thirsty but never satisfied.

Discussion Question: Why is an inaccurate portrait of Jesus so damaging?

Remember this: Jesus is God. He is the face of God (Heb. 1:2–3).

Jesus showed us what it was like to be holy, sinless, and righteous; intolerant of evil and sin; yet at the same time He was a perfect model of mercy, love, and forgiveness. Why do we struggle when we attribute these same characteristics to His Father? When Jesus was kind, that was God's kindness.

Key Point: God hates sin. He established laws to show us what sin is. People willingly disobey God and His law. The penalty for that is death. For you and me this is an unpayable debt. The only solution is a perfect sacrifice and someone to take our place. God loved YOU enough to send His son to die a brutal death on a cross in YOUR place. There was no other way we could be made right with God. That is the greatest act of love ever. This love is called **grace.**

Only people with part of the facts would interpret God as anything but incredibly loving. God allowed His only son to take the punishment on the cross for all mankind for their disobedience. In doing so He offered a way out of death, judgment, and separation from Him.

Remember when we talked about the fall of man in the garden? We mentioned that God would go to any extent to win back His kids. No cost was too high. He proved it.

On October 14, 1987, rescuers worked fifty-eight hours nonstop to free a little baby from an eight-inch well casing, where she was trapped twenty-two feet below the ground. She became known as Baby Jessica. New technology called waterjet cutting, was flown in to free her. A movie was even made about her story. No cost was spared to save this one little girl. The whole nation offered help to save her. When someone is lost, those who love them will do anything, no matter what the cost, to bring them home.

This story represents the type and depth of the God who loves you. He was not cruel to allow Christ to die; He was heartbroken and filled with grief, but made the ultimate sacrifice of love for **you,____.** Jesus, His Son, was the price He was willing to pay to rescue you!   (insert your name)

'Fess Up

- Have you questioned God's love for you because you didn't understand the whole story? Where did you get it wrong?

- How have you been guilty of creating a pocket-sized Jesus you can manage?

- How did it go with the action step this last week?

FLQA

"For God was pleased to have all his fullness dwell in him, and through him to reconcile to himself all things, whether things on earth or things in heaven, by making peace through his blood, shed on the cross."

Colossians 1:19–20

FACT	LESSON	QUESTION	ACTION

Pick an ACTION step to carry out this week and DO IT!

Key Question
How could a loving God allow His son to be brutally killed?

SOLITUDE. Spend five minutes quieting your heart and listening to God. Write here what He said:

Heart Psalm

Father, my heart before you today is:_____

It is like:

It is like:

Prayer for the Week

"Thank You, Father for loving me enough to send Your Son Jesus to take my place on the cross and bear the penalty for my sins. Help me to understand just how much You love me and what it cost You to rescue me."

LESSON 9

Where Will I Go When I Die?

Scripture: John 3:31–36

Key verse: John 3:36

"Whoever believes in the Son has eternal life, but whoever rejects the Son will not see life, for God's wrath remains on him."

Now I lay me down to sleep
I pray the Lord my soul to keep
If I should die before I wake
I pray the Lord my soul to take.

Children's bedtime prayer, eighteenth century

This is a very familiar prayer that parents often pray with their kids at bedtime. Even when someone dies, we explain to children that they went to heaven, and we will see them again someday. We tell them this because it provides comfort in the hurt of losing someone. Could this be true? Is it really that easy? Shouldn't I have to do something, like live a good life, care for the poor and needy, or give away my wealth? Well, it might be a bit more than this little prayer, but the truth is it's not complicated. Accepting God's free gift with a repentant heart is really all someone needs to gain heaven. **Jesus clearly explains eternal life is freely offered to anyone who just believes in Him.** John 3:36 says, *"Whoever believes in the Son has eternal life, but whoever rejects the Son will not see life, for God's wrath remains on Him."*

Remember in lesson 3 how we talked about how each person is a soul with a body? We know our body will someday pass away, but what about our soul? Our soul will live on forever, and it is important to know where that soul goes when your body dies. In John 11:25 Jesus said to the woman whose brother, Lazarus, had just died, *"I am the resurrection and the life. He who believes in me will live, even though he dies; and whoever believes in me will never die."* Jesus is talking about our soul living forever though our body is dead, and He shares with us that if you believe in Him, when your body dies your soul will live with Him forever.

There are many religions, preachers, and speakers who are eager to offer what our body craves. They may have charismatic leaders who will give speeches that make us feel better about ourselves, our circumstances, and this world. But it is only for a moment. The pull is strong, and we are often attracted to them because they teach what our ears want to hear and allow our hearts and thoughts to be indulged. It is easy to pay attention to all the things our bodies want. When we're hungry we eat; when we're tired we sleep. It is easy for us to understand our bodies and difficult to ignore its cries. The soul however is harder to understand; its hunger, and its need for rest are easier to ignore.

- Buddha was cremated; his ashes were divided up and buried.
- Confucius was buried in Qufu, China, among over one hundred thousand of his relatives.
- Ron Hubbard who founded Scientology had his ashes scattered in the ocean.
- Joseph Smith founded the Mormons. He was buried in his backyard.

You can go to the grave of every religious leader except one; Jesus Christ because He's the only one that rose from the grave. He's the only one that conquered death, the only one who validated that He was from God, the only one not defeated by death. Peter asked Jesus in John 6:68 (NLT), *"Lord, to whom would we go? You have the words that give eternal life."*

Imagine you are on a beach enjoying the surf when you are caught in a riptide. It drags you away from shore into death. You look and see two lifeguards sitting on their towers. They have had the exact same training. They have much of the same equipment. There's only one difference between them, one is dead and the other alive. Which one would you call for help? Which one would you have confidence in? Which one can save you and which one can't? Of course you would call out to the one that is alive to save you. This is why Jesus is different. **He is alive.** You can call on Him for eternal life.

God *does* promise according to 1 John 5:10–11, *"And this is Jesus's testimony; God has given us eternal life, and this life is in the Son. He who has the Son has life; he who does not have the Son of God does not have life!"* Eternal life is not a thing in and of itself; rather it is something that we receive because we have Jesus, who is eternal life. If we chose not to accept this eternal life, the alternative is eternal death apart from Him. John 3:16 tells us if we believe in Jesus Christ, God grants us eternal life. This being said, **life in the body will still have its challenges, difficulties, problems, and pain, but knowing our forever destination will provide hope that these challenges, difficulties, problems, and pain are all temporary**. Not only that, but God promises in Hebrews 13:5 *"I will never leave you or forsake you."* In other words He is with you in every situation. We don't have to live in these bodies alone waiting for heaven to be with God. He can be with you now.

Eternal life does not begin when you die. Eternal life begins at your life's conception, and while we are in this body, we have to choose whether to spend eternal life in heaven with God or in eternal hell separated from God. We can choose and know now, by faith, to believe in and have Jesus.

Key Point. Not only do we have eternal life, we have an eternal God with us every day in every circumstance. We are never alone.

'Fess Up

- **Are you afraid to die? Either way, what are your reasons?**

- According to the Bible, you either know or don't know where you will go when you die. Do you know? Can you live with your answer?

- How did it go with the action step this last week?

FLQA

"Whoever believes in the Son has eternal life, but whoever rejects the Son will not see life, for God's wrath remains on them."
John 3:36

FACT	LESSON	QUESTION	ACTION

Pick an ACTION step to carry out this week and DO IT!

Key Questions

What evidence does your life display that God is with you in all circumstances?

How does this evidence impact your view on where you will spend eternity?

SOLITUDE. Spend five minutes quieting your heart and listening to God. Write here what He said:

Heart Psalm

Father, my heart before you today is:_____

It is like:

It is like:

Prayer for the Week

"Father, I thank You for the offer of eternal life through Your son Jesus Christ. I also thank You for Your promise that You will always be with me, in this life, no matter what happens. Speak and meet with me today. Give me a love for You! In Jesus's name, Amen."

LESSON 10

What Do I Need to Do?

Scripture: Luke 18:18–32

Key Verses: Luke 18:18 (J. B. Phillips Translation)

"Then one of the Jewish rulers put this question to him, 'Master, I know that you are good; tell me, please, what must I do to be sure of eternal life?'"

If you too asked this question you would not be the first. Most people who entertain this question get the answer wrong, as did this man. Here was Jesus's response (paraphrase): *"You want to inherit eternal life? Obey every single one of the commandments!"*

As we have already discussed, no one has ever done that except Jesus (though in this story the rich man claimed that he had.) Jesus quickly points out that he loved money more than God, breaking the very first commandment: to love God first. (Exod. 20:3) Even if this was the only one he had broken, James 2:10 (NLT) says, *"For the person who keeps all of the laws except one is as guilty as a person who has broken all of God's laws."*

The first step in inheriting eternal life is admitting you're a lawbreaker, guilty of breaking God's law and without excuse. Romans 3:23 says, *"For all have sinned and fall short of the glory of God."* Admitting to being a lawbreaker is so much more than acknowledging doing wrong. It is seeing wrong the way God sees it. It means knowing you have broken His heart, and your heart is grieved in response.

As we've already addressed we have no right to alter, tinker with, or redefine God's law. We are tempted to do this when we believe the lie that if we lower God's standards we can better keep them but Deuteronomy 4:2 says, *"Do not add to what I command you and do not subtract from it, but keep the commands of the Lord your God that I give you."* Remember Jesus told the rich religious man, "You must obey all of the law." He was told this by Jesus, God's Son, the only one who has ever kept God's law perfectly.

The next step in inheriting eternal life is to believe what Jesus says. In Acts 16: 30–31 a prison guard asks, *"What must I do to be saved?"* The disciples replied, *"Believe in the Lord Jesus Christ, and you will be saved, you and your household."*

Reviewing what we have studied so far and keeping in mind our need to believe what the Bible says:

- God is the creator of the world.
- Man rebelled against God and broke His law.
- This caused a closed door between God and man.
- Every man since has continued to break God's law.
- The punishment for this is death and hell.

- Jesus lived a perfect life in complete obedience to God's law.
- He is a worthy sacrifice in our place on the cross to appease God's wrath against our sin.

Sounds simple, just believe. But how often do we struggle to believe or trust others? How many times have we been hurt and it prevents us from believing truth. Our past pains can block our heart from accepting this free gift. The good news is, because of **Jesus being perfect, He can never hurt us;** He can only love, love abundantly, and always keep His promises. Believing in Him is unlike any other relationship we can ever know. It cannot be compared.

Now if you admit you are a sinner and believe in Jesus Christ, **the next thing you need to do is to accept the free gift of eternal life and salvation God again extends to you, because of His grace.** Grace is God's love for us even though we don't deserve it. Ephesians 2:8–9 says, "*For it is by grace you have been saved through faith—and this is not from yourselves, it is the gift of God—not by works, so that no one can boast.*"

In other words, to accept God's forgiveness and eternal life, you must lay down the thought that there is anything you have done or could do to earn God's forgiveness. It's an undeserved gift. To inherit eternal life, you must accept from God something you could never earn or deserve: His forgiveness. And you must receive it personally. Many people come to Jesus thinking they have everything they need to please Him, but do not realize their complete failure to keep God's law. Isaiah 64:6 tells us that, "all our righteous acts are like filthy rags." The person whom God accepts is the one who comes to Him admitting their complete failure in keeping His law, admitting they have nothing to offer Him and are in need of saving.

Finally Acts 2:38 says, "*Repent and be baptized every one of you, in the name of Jesus Christ for the forgiveness of your sins. And you will receive the gift of the Holy Spirit.*"

You must repent. This simply means telling God you are willing to turn your back on all the things that you have said and done that have broken His heart and His law. It means turning to God and now seeking to live a life of obedience to the God who loves you and who can give you the ability to obey Him.

You must be baptized. To be baptized is to follow in obedience for the first time. When you are baptized you are stating to the world, your friends, and your family that you are now a Christian. In baptism a person is submerged completely under water and then lifted up out of the water. It symbolizes when Christ was put in the grave after He died on the cross. When Jesus was buried, we are under water; all of your sins are buried with Him. When Jesus rose from the grave, He left all of your sins in hell and your punishment was paid. So when you come out of the water, it symbolizes your coming out of the grave with Him, now clean and perfect in God's sight.

You must receive the Holy Spirit. Simply put, Jesus's spirit comes and lives inside of you, giving you the ability to be made more and more like Him every day. And what example did Jesus leave for us? He obeyed God His Father, and He will help you do the same. This is the evidence that He's alive in your life!

You will likely meet many who claim they are Christians; they know of the life of Jesus and what He did; they may even believe in Him saving them from their sins but they have no desire to obey God. Something is missing. Is this you? In God's words; 1 John 2:3–5 says, "*We know that we have come to know Him IF (emphasis mine) we obey His commands. Whoever says, 'I know Him,' but does not do what He commands is a liar, and the truth is not in that person. But if anyone obeys His word, love for God is truly made complete in them. This is how we know we are in Him.*"

You must forgive. Read Matthew 18:21–35. Here Jesus teaches that once we have experienced God's patience and forgiveness, we are to freely share it with anyone who has hurt us. Jesus tells us to be one of His followers. We are to show the forgiveness we have received from Him to others. If we refuse, if we have no desire to forgive those who have hurt us, we will find ourselves distant from God. He forgave us though we were totally unworthy of forgiveness. We are to do the same! When you struggle to forgive, just remember He has forgiven you on the cross, and if you ask He can give you the ability to forgive anyone.

Romans 6:22 says, *"But now that you have been set free from sin and have become slaves of God, the benefit you reap leads to holiness, and the result is eternal life."* Likewise there cannot be a Christian who receives from God forgiveness, salvation, and eternal life without also taking the other end of the stick which is obedience to God and His Word and offering these things freely to others.

'Fess Up

- **Have you been guilty of wanting from God His love, forgiveness, and all the benefits of being a Christian, with no commitment to becoming a follower of Jesus and one who seeks to live a life of obedience to His word? (This is a very important question. Don't move past it quickly!) Check one: ☐ Yes ☐ No**

- **How do you think a kind, yet holy God would respond to your answer?**

- **How did it go with the action step this last week?**

FLQA

"For it is by grace you have been saved, through faith and not from yourselves, it is the gift of God—not by works, so that no one can boast. For we are God's workmanship, created in Christ Jesus to do good works, which God prepared in advance for us to do."

Ephesians 2:8–10

FACT	LESSON	QUESTION	ACTION

Pick an ACTION step to carry out this week and DO IT!

Key Question
What must I do to inherit eternal life?

SOLITUDE. Spend five minutes quieting your heart and listening to God. Write here what He said:

Heart Psalm

Father, my heart before you today is:_____

It is like:

It is like:

Brad Ringer

Prayer for the Week

"Father, forgive me. Forgive me for my selfishness. Help me to see how loving and generous You are especially for sending Jesus Christ Your son to die on the cruel cross in my place; for my lawbreaking, for my sin. Thank You, thank You, thank You. I love you. In Jesus's name, Amen."

LESSON 11

How Do I Stay Right with God?

Scriptures: 2 Corinthians 5:11–21

Key Verses: 2 Corinthians 5:17–19

"Therefore, if anyone is in Christ, he is a new creation; the old has gone, the new has come! All this is from God, who reconciled us to himself through Christ and gave us the ministry of reconciliation; that God was reconciling the world to himself in Christ, not counting men's sins against them. And He has committed to us the message of reconciliation."

If Jesus makes me right with God, how do I stay right with God even when I blow it and break his law again and sin?

When God saves, resurrects, or transforms a soul, it is an act of genesis, because He has to create something out of nothing; He has to animate something that is dead. So, breathing new life into a spiritually dead soul is the same as when he breathed life into Adam.

Second Corinthians 5:21 says, *"God made Him who had no sin to be sin for us, so that in Him we might become the righteousness of God."* Simply what this means is that when Christ died on the cross, He took all of your sin, guilt and judgment, and punishment for you. He took all of these things from you and in exchange, gave you His righteousness, His goodness, His right standing with His father…the great exchange. Once you have been made right with God through Jesus Christ, you don't have to *stay right* with God because you *are right* with God permanently. This happens because of what Jesus Christ did for you. Does this mean we have license to sin, and it will be okay because we're already forgiven? No, but rather Christ in us (the Holy Spirit) helps us and gives us a desire to live without sin, a desire that was never there before salvation. We as humans will always be stubborn, but we can know God's kindness and continual forgiveness.

The Bible says, "If any man be in Christ he is a new creature," meaning one whose sins were dealt with on the cross and who now lives in a right standing with God. This person can live every day fully committed to Christ by seeking to live lives of obedience to Him. How? They have confidence that they are permanently reconciled with God. They rest in the fact that they are both pardoned and forgiven through the cross. They count God as a friend, because they have a deep appreciation for what Christ did for them, dying in their place. When you truly grasp what Christ did, it will drive you to please Him and hate sin! This is something God does through you, not a result of your own attempts.

Consider this analogy. You are on the crew of a great ship. The crew, yourself included mutinies and rebels against your captain even though he is a great man. Because of this uprising, there is an explosion leaving fiery wreckage where once was your ship. You find yourself swimming in icy cold water, alone and exhausted, feeling the weight of your arms, so tired and heavy as you try desperately to swim for shore. The knowledge that your life is about to end washes over you with the waves, the undertow pulling you to a certain death. Just as you resign to your fate, you feel the strong hands of the captain you rebelled against pull you to safety. He lays you across the beam he had been clinging to, a beam with room only for one. You watch as buffeted by the waves, he slips beneath the cold dark sea.

The captain is Christ who died in our place. He died *because* of our rebellion, yet he loved us enough to exchange places with us and save our lives. **Do you know of anyone, who would be so willing to die for you?**

By faith, through God's amazing grace and through the work of the Holy Spirit, those who are saved are compelled by Christ's love to no longer live for themselves. They now desire to live pure for God, evidencing daily lives that have been reconciled with the holy God, the loving Father. They also seek to take the reconciliation they have experienced and share it with everyone they meet, that others too can be made right with God. Once you know this joy personally, you can't help but want to tell others about it.

Key Point: A right relationship with God is never based on what you do. It is based on what Christ did for you on the cross. Jesus was a loving and innocent substitute who took the punishment for every sin you have ever committed. Because of your sin, Jesus experienced alienation from God. He stood condemned for your sin. He faced hell, friendlessness, conviction, and death. He was abandoned and humiliated when He took on your sins, all because He loved you.

Sadly the church today is filled with many unconverted "believers." These are people who believe a lot of the right things about Jesus, but they're not changed by it. Their lives are not made new. The knowledge stays in their head, but never makes its way to their heart. They're not transformed into people who live and act like they are reconciled to God. It's because they never allowed the Holy Spirit to take all their sin and guilt and place it on Christ on the cross, where it was put to death or never embraced the truth that Jesus's right standing with God was transferred to them.

There are three types of "Christians":

- Fake ones
- Halfhearted ones
- Fully committed ones

Discussion Question: Be honest. Which are you?

First Thessalonians 4:7–8 says, *"For God did not call us to be impure, but to live a holy life. Therefore, anyone who rejects their instruction does not reject a human being but God, the very God who gives you his Holy Spirit."*

Does this sound like you? Does it sound like the Christians you know? Think on this. Does it sound right that God would make us into new creatures just so we would become old again and return to our lives of rebellion and sin? These are the very things that put His son Jesus on the cross.

Discussion Question: Have you ever admitted your sin and guilt and asked God to exchange it for Jesus's righteousness and right standing with your Heavenly Father?

'Fess Up

- Have you ever asked God to take all your sin away, to put it on Christ and the cross, and "restock" your heart with Jesus's righteousness, goodness, and love?

- What does being "made new" look like?

- How did it go with the action step this last week?

FLQA

"Therefore, if anyone is in Christ, he is a new creation; the old has gone, the new has come! All this is from God, who reconciled us to himself through Christ and gave us the ministry of reconciliations; that God was reconciling the world to himself in Christ, not counting men's sins against them. And he has committed to us the message of reconciliation."

II Corinthians 5:17–19

FACT	LESSON	QUESTION	ACTION

Pick an ACTION step to carry out this week and DO IT!

Key Questions

If Jesus makes you right with God, how do you stay right with Him even when you blow it and sin?

Do you have to be a perfect Christian? Why or why not?

SOLITUDE. Spend five minutes quieting your heart and listening to God. Write here what He said:

Heart Psalm

Father, my heart before you today is:_____

It is like:

It is like:

Prayer for the Week

"Father, I believe that on the cross, Your son Jesus took all of my sin, guilt, and shame and crucified it. I also believe in the great exchange, that You in turn have placed on me: His goodness and purity. I know this for a fact, so help me live up to it by the power of Your Holy Spirit. I love You. In Jesus's name, Amen."

LESSON 12

First Love

Scripture: Luke 9:18–27

Key Verse: Luke 9:23–24

"Then He said to them all: 'If anyone would come after me, he must deny himself and take up his cross daily and follow me. For whoever wants to save his life will lose it, but whoever loses his life for me will save it.'"

This is a very important topic. It is also a very sensitive one. Jesus said in this passage of Scripture that unless a man or woman denies the self, he or she cannot be one of His disciples. Anyone who gets on this Christian journey, thinking it is only, "give me, give me, give me" and "get, get, get" does not have a valid contract with God. One of the foundational principles that Jesus laid out in becoming a Christian is that to follow Him, you would have to deny yourself. What does this mean? It is turning away from things you lust after, put before God, and things that are offensive to God, His law and His word. These are the very things for which Jesus died.

With God it is all or nothing. He gave the life of His own son to die for you. What more could you give to prove to Him your love? He gave His all. When you gave your life to Christ, did you give Him your all: your body, your lusts, your relationships, your will, your attitudes, your dreams, or your very life? Isaac Watts once wrote in his hymn *When I Survey the Wondrous Cross*, "Love so amazing, so divine, demands my heart, my life, my all."

Key Point: You cannot have a valid contract with God and live for yourself.

Romans 6:22–23 says: *"But now you have been set free from sin and have become slaves to God, the benefit you reap leads to holiness, and the result is eternal life. For the wages of sin is death, but the gift of God is the eternal life in Christ Jesus our Lord."*

We have all come across Christians who are miserable people. They think they can have all the benefits Jesus offers, forgiveness, answered prayer, eternal life, prosperity, etc., but go on living in a manner that does not honor Him. They have forgotten or become numb to what Jesus did for them. This is completely unacceptable to God and will keep them from ever truly encountering Him. If this bothers you, perhaps you too **have forgotten what Christ did for you. It would be wise to review your contract with God and find out what you agreed to in the first place...what being a Christian really means.**

Having Jesus as your First Love

1. **Means obeying God your Master,** even if you don't like what God asks or requires, or even understand it. If God loves us so much to send His only Son to die for us, can we not trust Him even if we don't always

understand? First John 5:3 says, *"This is love for God: to obey His commands. And His commands are not burdensome."*

2. **Requires you to be loyal to God your friend**. Jesus said this in John 15:13, *"Greater love has no one than this, that he lay down his life for his friends."* He was loyal enough to you to die for you. Are you loyal enough to live for Him? It is understood friends have their friends' backs. Are you loyal to Jesus when He is mocked? Does it bother you when people misuse His name? Can you deny your own comfort and safety to stand up for Him? This is what a friend would do.

3. **Requires that you respect God your Father above everybody in every situation**. This means to be fully committed to obeying and honoring God and His word, *no matter what the cost is to you personally*. It may be the cost of friends or family. Luke 14:26 says, *"If anyone comes to me and does not hate his father and mother, wife and children, brothers and sisters—yes, even their own life—such a person cannot be my disciple."* It means you may love your family, but you love God more.

4. **Requires faithfulness to God as your lover**. To put God first and to keep Him first in all that you do. To have His needs above your own needs, wishes, and desires. This is denying yourself for Him.

I was performing a wedding ceremony once and during the ceremony, I asked the best man for the rings. He handed them to me. I held them in my hand for a moment and then threw them as hard as I could into the sanctuary. You could hear everybody gasp. After a dramatic pause, I reached into my pocket and pulled out the real rings. I looked at the bride and groom and those in attendance and said, "People take the marriage contract symbolized by these rings too lightly. In our culture and in the church, people too quickly discard these rings and the commitment behind them. You were all shocked when I threw the rings, but are you equally shocked when people throw them away to get divorced?"

It can be a real temptation to take our commitment to God too casually, but God does not enter into a relationship with you casually. Again it cost Him the life of His son. Jesus is fully committed to you. When you come into a relationship with God, He expects you to be fully committed too. If you're not, you do not have a valid contract with God.

That doesn't mean that we don't make mistakes or struggle at times in our relationship with God. What it does mean, is that when we do disobey God, fail to stick up for Him, disrespect His law or will, or put other things before Him, we quickly come back to Him and confess it and make things right with Him. This heart to always be right with God is proof that our contract is intact.

First John 1:9 says, *"If we confess our sins, He is faithful and just to forgive us our sins and to cleanse us from all our unrighteousness."*

God is always faithful to forgive you for whatever you have done. But what is your responsibility? Your part of the contract requires that you go to God, you confess, and you walk with Him.

This reminds me of a number of years ago when I was very ill. For three years I did not sleep for more than an hour or two a night. I experienced constant dizziness. I struggled constantly with anxiety, depression, and loneliness. The days were long and hard, the nights even more so. I felt hopeless and lost especially when the doctors could not find out what was wrong with me. One night after years of this pain, I was again wide awake and crying. I was convinced this was now my life, and because of it I was going to die. With nothing left to hold onto, I cried to God and said, "I give you my wife Robin. I give you my two daughters Bonnie and Laura. I know you will take good care of them. Here is my life. It is yours!" With that I heard the Lord quietly say, "That's all I ever wanted!"

God simply wants all of you!

'Fess Up

- **Is there anything specific that is keeping you from total surrender to Christ as your First Love?**

- **What areas of your life have you not turned over to God? Why?**

- **How did you do with the action step this last week?**

FLQA

"Then he said to them all, "If anyone would come after me, he must deny himself and take up his cross daily and follow me. For whoever wants to save his life will lose it, but whoever loses his life for me will save it.'"

Luke 9:23–24

FACT	LESSON	QUESTION	ACTION

Pick an ACTION step to carry out this week and DO IT!

Key Question
What will having Christ as my First Love look like?

SOLITUDE. Spend five minutes quieting your heart and listening to God. Write here what He said:

Prayer for the Week

"Father God. I am sorry for all the times I've been selfish before You, always wanting You to do things for me, while I refused to obey You. I am sorry, please forgive me. Change my heart. Take my whole life. I want to be wholly Yours. I know that You signed my contract with You with Christ's blood. I honor that sacrifice now, by giving my whole life to You as my Lord and Savior. In Jesus's name, Amen."

About the Author

Brad Ringer is the founder of Pure for God Ministries Inc. He is called to preach, teach, encourage, exhort, express God's love, and speak the truth in love to people.

Brad has been a youth evangelist, speaker, preacher, teacher and youth communicator. He attended Nyack Christian and Missionary Alliance College. Brad has served as both a youth pastor and senior pastor. He was the Executive Director for the Buffalo Christian Center in Buffalo, NY, and former Chairman on the Board of Education for Charles Grandison Finney High School. Brad has also served as an NFL chaplain to several teams.

He created "The Handwritten Bible," an evangelistic tool for churches for use in reaching their communities. Brad has directed over twenty missions to the United Kingdom and for the last several years has partnered with Southwest Youth Ministries (SWYM) in England, serving as a teacher at their annual training conference for youth and lay workers.

Brad and his wife Robin reside in Cape Vincent, New York.

To request more copies of this workbook, please contact:
Pure for God Ministries Inc.
PO Box 965
Cape Vincent, New York 13618
716.674.0611
pureforgod@ymail.com
www.pureforgod.org